GRANT WRITING

Developing a culture of
resource development
for your non profit

101

Dr. William P. Clark

GRANT WRITING

101

Developing a culture of resource development for your nonprofit

AUTHOR:

DR. WILLIAM CLARK

Printed in the United States of America
First Printing, 2019

Willis Dawson Publishing House
PO Box 193
Windsor, CT 06095

Table of Contents

SECTION 1: BEFORE YOU APPLY

CHAPTER 1 – A CLEAR ORGANIZATIONAL STRATEGY

Before you apply for a grant, have a clear organizational strategy. An organizational strategy is the blueprint to sell your organization's plans to execute its work and the specific steps it will and will not take to ensure very specific outcomes. Every organization needs an organizational strategy to ensure every member of the team knows the map to the desired destination of the organization (ie: goals). When there is no map to guide every member of the team, members will arrive at a destination that may not be the one identified or designated by organizational leaders.

An organizational strategy takes into account the critical steps that must occur in order for the organization to achieve success. While there are various formats of what organizational strategies look like; the basic framework of an organizational strategy includes (1) major tasks, (2) subtasks, (3) start dates,

(4) due dates, (5) owners of tasks, (6) status of each task, and (7) notes. As I said before, there are various ways to display strategic plans or organizational strategies, but these are the common ingredients found within.

I should note here that a higher-level organizational strategy may not include all these components but may include the following core content. That content includes (1) where we are now, (2) where we want to be, (3) how we get where we want to be, (4) what steps we want to take to get where we want to be, and (5) how we measure our progress. Within foundations (grant givers), an organizational strategy can be characterized as an organizational theory of change. Again, there are various templates as to following core content. That content includes where we are now, where we want to be, how we get where we want to be, what steps we want to take to get where we want to be, and how we measure our progress.

Within the nonprofit arena, an organizational strategy can be characterized by foundations as an organizational theory of change. Again, there are various templates as to what an organizational theory of change looks like but the basic content is inclusive of one or more of the elements I just outlined.

The other critical reason for the necessity of an organizational strategy is, a foundation may want to know your plan or strategic direction and how their money will be used to advance your organization toward that direction and meet its goals. It's very difficult and time consuming to put together a rushed strategic or organizational plan in order to meet the needs of a potential funder. A healthy organization will have an active organizational plan in place that articulates the strategy of the organization and is shareable at any given time so that funders, stakeholders, and partners will have a clear idea as to what your organization wants to accomplish.

The other reason it's vital to have an organizational strategy is so you and your leadership team can make clear and sound decisions as to which funders may be a good fit for your organization. A nonprofit that is starting out is hungry to acquire as many grants as possible. Organizations that are struggling financially are hungry to acquire as many grants as possible. However, one of the ways nonprofit organizations tie their hands and limit their effectiveness is by acquiring too many grants that do not align with their organizational strategy. Some grants are not relevant or helpful to your organization, even if the funding is significant. If the funding source is requesting a new organization to complete a project that is completely out of the skill set and competency of the organization, it will detract from the organization's effectiveness and take away from the organization's ability to have its desired impact on the lives of its target client. To avoid such conflict, it's imperative for nonprofits to understand their strategy and find the funders or investors who align with their strategy to make it a reality. Note: not all money is good money.

CHAPTER 2 - CLEAR PURPOSE ON HOW TO SPEND MONEY

Aligned with a clear organizational strategy is a clear purpose for how the money will be used if awarded to your organization. The way to know how money will be used is to have a clear and useful organizational strategy. The strategy will outline the critical tasks and goals that the organization needs to accomplish. Funding sources are nothing more than injections of resources to help you achieve the goals and check off tasks on your strategy document. From this point, you can develop an organizational budget that supports the execution of your organizational strategy.

For example, if your organization has a focus on ending homelessness and you develop a three point strategy that says homelessness will be ended by (1) conducting thorough research of all homeless individuals within your city or a defined region, (2) working with legislators to develop legislation that changes how homeless individuals are cared for by our society, and (3) providing counseling and a case management apparatus to provide direct and personalized support for individuals so they can ultimately develop a customized plan that will resolve their personal issues around homelessness. Of course, your organizational plan will have a number of subtasks and, perhaps, additional sub tasks to articulate how the organization will reach its goal.

But we are trying to answer the question of how to create a clear purpose for how the money will be spent. Let's take, for example, the development of a database to track all the homeless people in the region. In order to develop the database, the organization must first hire a developer who will develop the system and purchase computers, software, internet access, and office space. These and many more resources are needed to ensure that your organization has the capacity to develop an information database to track all homeless individuals within the region. Now, when the organization applies for funding to support their strategic direction, and a particular funder supports capacity building projects that will advance an organizations ability to do its work, you can point to this organizational strategy and say that we can use the funds to support the development of the database system by paying for the specific items that will support the developer and the eventual production of the platform that will manage all data collected.

In many cases, a budget will be requested along with a grant application. In addition, funders will request a budget narrative to accompany the budget. A budget narrative is an explanation of every line item that is identified within the budget. For example, you may be asked to identify the staff salaries. Within the budget narrative, you will be asked to explain the role of each staff member and their impact on this specific project. For the example we gave above about the development of a database that tracks all homeless individuals, you would enter a salary for the developer of the system and the cost for each supply item the developer will need to do the job. You will then provide a budget narrative, or an explanation for the budget, so that the reader of the application will have a better understanding as to why you're asking for the amount that's in your budget and why you dedicated a line item within your budget to a person or supplies associated with the project.

Use the budget narrative as an opportunity to simplify how readers of your application can better understand your proposed program and strategy. Every opportunity that is presented to you to write and further explain something about your program should be maximized. Remember, most - if not all - grant applications have a word limit. Something like the budget narrative may not have a word limit. This is a hidden gem in the grant application that offers a good opportunity to share more about your organization and your proposal. Remember, the basic purpose of the budget narrative is to explain the purpose of each expense on the budget sheet. Do not lose sight of this in spite of the temptation to go off topic.

CHAPTER 3 - WHO HAS THE MONEY

Before you apply for a grant, find out who has the money. Let me be more specific; find out who has money slated to support programs like yours? Finding the correct money source is important before you spend any amount of time completing a grant application. The worst thing you can do is waste your time completing a grant application and later come to find out your organization is not qualified. Even mature nonprofits sometimes fall into the trap of completing a grant application they are not qualified for.

The reason organizations submit applications they are not qualified for has mainly to do with a couple of key factors that include the following:

- A need for money
- An unfocused or unclear strategy or plan
- Not paying attention to the requirements of the grant application

It's important to pay attention to the small details when you pursue a grant, and that includes limiting the grants you apply for to only grants that strategically align with your organization's strategy, mission, values, beliefs, etc. What you are looking for is alignment.

It matters - a lot - that standards are established for the grants you pursue for your nonprofit. These standards will limit the amount of time you waste completing grant applications that do not align with the organization. These standards will also help the organization learn how to say no to applications that serve as more of a distraction than an aid. Let's explore this further.

There will come a time when your organization will perform well, and funders will approach your organization with an invitation to submit a grant application. When this happens, just know that this will make you and other key leaders in the organizations feel good. An invitation to submit a funding application is one of the most significant signs of respect a nonprofit can receive. However, some invitations should not result in the submission of an application. Why? For the same reasons we discussed before...if the funding does not align with the goals of your organization, the organization will ultimately suffer and pay the ultimate price of being labeled as a non-performer and will not receive an invitation to apply for funding from the same funder again or for some time.

Finding who has the money may also require you or members of your team to network. Sometimes, finding money may come at a party or at an event hosted by a competitor or a strategic partner. Even attending events of organizations that you were not familiar with can kindle some interesting results. At some of these events, you will find funders, investors, stakeholders, or future partners who can point you in the right direction where the money may exist. Do not be shy about attending these events. Come to these events prepared to talk about your organization and promote what you can provide. You may find that some or all the services provided by your organization are an attractive thing to a funder or provider. Do not hold back when given the opportunity to share your story. It's that one little detail you decide to share that will capture the attention or ear of someone who is in the middle of completing an application and needs a partner or someone who's looking to give away money. There are times foundations have to meet a quota of grants given, and your organization provides that source. You may meet someone who is looking to donate money because they have some money to give away before the tax or fiscal year is out. You never know where the money may come from. Be ready at all times.

CHAPTER 4 - HOW ARE YOU GOING TO GET THE JOB DONE

L et me make a clear point here, funders have specific funding expectations that come with receiving their funding. Because nonprofits, particularly organizations that are starting out, are desperate to receive grant resources to get operations off the ground, they do not pay attention to what the funder is asking for in return for the money.

For example, a funder that provides funding support for youth programming will garner a lot of attention from nonprofits that serve young adults. Out of desperation, you apply for the grant thinking you can meet the goals but you miss the details of the scope of work and the expectations of the funder. For example, this funder may expect the winning recipients to accomplish the following:

- Serve 200 young adults in a specific neighborhood
- Qualified young adults must be justice involved

- 90% of Young adults must complete a diversionary training program and must show evidence of personal life change and completion of the proposed program
- 75% of young adults must be placed in a skills training program or employment
- Employment wages must be $12 per hour or more
- 60% of young adults must be retained for 12 months or longer in their employment
- All data must be maintained in a viable database
- Quarterly reports must be completed
- 60% of staff must attend annual training events provided by the funder
- This funder is willing to award 3 organizations $600k each over a 3-year period ($200K PER YEAR)

Mature nonprofits are used to expectations like the ones I just laid out. However, if your organization is a start-up or is small and desperate for funding, these requirements will seem foreign. Even if these expectations do not seem foreign, many organizations misjudge their own capacity to meet these standards because their eyes are so focused on the $600k. That $600k will pay overhead, rent, salaries, etc. Essentially, this $600k is a life saver for your organization. While the $600k is a life saver, it can also be the death of your organization if your organization is unable to meet the demands/goals of the funder or is unable to maintain data integrity. Further, if these requirements are outside the goals and competency of your organization, you will spend more time trying to satisfy the scope of work for this funder and take away from what your organization does well. Doing this will harm the culture of your organization and brand your organization as unfit to perform and deliver on grant commitments.

While it may not feel good in the moment to turn down opportunities to further fund, sustain, and support your nonprofit, you are actually saving its reputation and maintaining its health by turning money down. Perhaps the bright side to turning down money for the right reasons is an opportunity for the organization to further define its purpose or build its capacity to compete for such grants in the near future.

CHAPTER 5 - LEVERAGING FUNDING

Before you apply for a grant, think about opportunities available to your organization for leveraging funding from other sources. The question you're probably asking me is, "What does it mean to leverage funding?" Leveraging funding means the following:

> "Leverage is all about finding ways to do more with existing human and financial resources. Since money is limited, efficiency is necessary. Leveraged non-profits find ways to reduce or maintain operational costs while increasing their service to people in need. To make that happen, money cannot be wasted, and it can't be the answer to every challenge. Partners and volunteers have to be employed to meet the mission."[1]

The key to understanding this definition is, "Finding ways to do more with existing human and financial resources." In layman's terms, for every $1 a nonprofit spends, leveraged funds - funds influenced or indirectly controlled by the nonprofit - can be mobilized as a 1-for-1 match or higher. For example:

A case study for leveraging funds. A funder has released a $1 million grant to serve homeless individuals. Services provided must include:

1. Identifying where they are
2. Getting them into a shelter
3. Providing case management, and
4. Providing rapid re-housing.

A nonprofit that provides homeless services will spend $500k on case management services and food for individuals who are served at the local shelter. However, the funder requests that, in the scope of work, service providers must also provide rapid re-housing for the individuals who are served. The problem with this is, this particular nonprofit (let's call the nonprofit The Homeless Nonprofit) does not provide housing solutions for homeless individuals. The Homeless Nonprofit mission is to collect data on homeless individuals in the region and provide case management support for homeless individuals. Their mission and their work do not include providing housing or housing support or housing subsidy. Despite the specific services provided by The Homeless Nonprofit and their desire to pursue funding offered by this funder, The Homeless Nonprofit knows it cannot provide housing.

The remedy to this challenge is for The Homeless Nonprofit to leverage resources from partners who can provide what they cannot. In this scenario, leveraging resources looks like this. The Homeless Nonprofit continues to collect and manage data and provide ongoing case management services. To meet the goals of the funder to provide rapid re-housing, The Homeless Nonprofit decides to partner with the local Public Housing Agency, two private landlords, the city where it operates, and three local shelters. Why? The local Public Housing has committed to make 20 affordable housing units along with 10 Section 8 vouchers available for homeless individuals served by The Homeless Nonprofit. Two private landlords have committed to make five units each available from their housing portfolio to be used by Section 8 voucher holders. The city has committed to provide funds to cover the tenant portion of the rent for public housing and Section 8. The three emergency shelters have committed to providing 10 beds each to immediately house clients that are referred by The Homeless Nonprofit. The commitment from all the partners amounts to the support of 30 clients. Lastly, The Homeless Nonprofit will either hire interns, a local homeless tracking agency, or a regional expert to find all homeless individuals.

The 30 clients that will be served by The Homeless Nonprofit and its strategic partners meets the goals of the funder. Further, The Homeless Nonprofit now has the leveraged capacity and resources to apply for this $1M grant. Before applying for this grant, The Homeless Nonprofit did not have the capacity or resources to apply alone. However, after evaluating its strategic partners, The Homeless Nonprofit determined that if they could leverage their partnerships, they would have more than enough resources, skills, and staff to meet goals provided in the scope of work for this $1M dollar grant.

Note, the strategy I just outlined applies to grants that are small or large. Be thoughtful about how leveraged resources can be used to pursue new funding. The key to being effective in developing partnerships is identifying the core competency of your organization. Doing this allows you to determine where and how partners can plug in to a proposal.

CHAPTER 6 - PLAN EVERY STEP OF THE PROCESS

Many nonprofits, including mature ones, shoot themselves in the foot when it comes to applying for grant opportunities because of the absence of an action plan that outlines the steps that must (or should) be taken to complete a quality and well thought out grant application. When a new grant application becomes available, most nonprofits stop what they are doing and begin to complete the application. This type of response often leads to ignoring the importance of a few key internal behavioral disciplines that should be active within every organization. Those behaviors are the inclusion of the relevant thought leaders who will contribute to the development of the grant, an evaluation of all grants to determine its relevancy to the organization strategy, an action plan to govern the development of all key components of a grant, and a conversation with all strategic partners to ensure their support and to ensure the development of a MOU if it is required. An action plan is important for the development of a grant application.

Another reason it's important to plan every step of the process is, some funders require prospective funders to attend a bidder's conference. The bidder's conference is used by the funder to explain the specific processes and expectations the funder has about the application process to applicants. During the bidder's conference, applicants are able to ask specific questions about the process and the application, itself. This is your time to gain an advantage for your application. You can also observe which organizations are represented in the room so you can size up your competition. However, if you miss the bidder's conference, you will lose the opportunity to apply for the grant.

Another reason it's important to plan every step of the process is, most larger grants - particularly those grants that are local to your base of operations - require specific directions for delivery and binding. For example, here are the final directions from a local funder.

Sample directions from funder A.

The proposer is solely responsible for assuring that anything sent to funder A arrives safely and on time. Any submission to funder A, including inquiries regarding the RFP, and/or proposals not received at either the specified place and/or by the specified date and time will be rejected and returned to the proposer unopened by funder A. Proposals must be submitted in accordance the scope of work provided.

- Proposals should be submitted on 8½ by 11-inch paper, with one-inch margins using 12-point Arial font.

- One original proposal and ten (10) copies must be submitted; the original must be signed in blue ink.

- At least one copy of the proposal should be in loose-leaf form, that is, not stapled or bound and easily accessible for photocopying.

- Proposers must also submit an electronic copy of the proposal as a single PDF file that contains the entire proposal, in the same order as the hard copy, and a separate file in MS Excel 97 or higher containing the budget.

- Funder A will NOT pay for any expenses incurred prior to the execution of a contract or issuance of a formal Letter of Intent.

- Please be advised that funder A monitors all programs at least once during a contract period. Contractors may be required to provide documentation of expenses as related to the negotiated budget. Proposals may be withdrawn by written notice. Withdrawals will be accepted at any time up to execution of a contract.

- Proposers are required to submit one (1) original proposal signed in blue ink, 10 paper copies and one electronic copy.

- Issuance of this RFP is coordinated by staff member A (below would be their contact information).

These instructions are specific and must be followed to their exact specifications. Following instructions alone can win opportunities for you when other organizations fail to do so or miss the little details. I encourage you to include the details of such specifications in your action plan as you planned out every step join the grant writing process. These details are not too small or too minuscule to ignore. A good action plan or project plan articulates the very little details that will make the difference in this successful completion of a project.

Do not ignore these instructions; they are created for a reason. In many cases, these instructions exist so that reviewers can assess each application assigned to them in a systematic order. If your application process ignores or does not follow the directions provided by the funder, the funder has every right - and will likely use this right - to disqualify your application without giving it a review. This helps them reduce the workload in reviewing so many applications. Don't be one of the nonprofit organizations that loses out on opportunities because you and your team refuse to plan out every step of the process and refused to follow the instructions provided by funders.

Another reason it's important to plan every step of the application process is, a funder may require a letter of intent (LOI) to filter out applicants who will not move forward with the application process. If your LOI is not accepted, you will not be invited to complete a full grant application. Suffice it to say, it is extremely important that you put effort into the development of a letter of intent and follow the instructions provided by the funder when writing the letter. If a letter of intent is required by a funder and the funder does not provide any instructions, be sure to research best practices and standards when drafting a letter of intent. In some cases, the funder may suggest or state that a letter of intent should not be greater than three pages. In other cases, a funder many say that they only want a one or two paragraph letter expressing your interest. Remember, the letter of intent is intended to filter out grant applications. There will be moments that a funder will already have organizations in mind with whom they want to move forward in the process. If your organization is favored by a funder, a simple letter of intent will push your application process forward; however, you must complete the letter of intent. There will be other cases where the organization may not be favored by the funder for whatever reason, but the letter of intent is an opportunity for your organization to change the mind of a funder. I will mention here that sometimes a letter of intent plus a phone call can do wonders in changing the mind or perspective a funder may have of your organization. Be strategic and smart about the process. Hence, we are talking about planning the process out before beginning the application process.

Completing a winning grant application that can be used repeatedly takes time, planning, and feedback. To get to that desired end, please embrace this key piece of advice. DO NOT RUSH THE GRANT APPLICATION PROCESS. There will be instances when a funder will release a grant application with a one-week turn around requirement. There will be instances when your organization will not find out about a grant application opportunity until the very last minute. There will be times when you will have more than enough time to complete a grant application. No matter the circumstances your organization is facing, it is important not to rush the grant application process.

Use as much time as you need to complete a grant application.

SECTION 2 - PREPARING GRANT APPLICATIONS

CHAPTER 7 - HAVE A CLEAR STRATEGY FOR THE PROCESS

Having a clear strategy is different from planning every step of the grant application process. What I mean by having a clear strategy is, your organization has a clear understanding about what it is applying for, why it is applying for those funds, and how it will frame its perspective about why your organization should be funded above others. This represents the strategy of the organization. It is not enough for your organization to simply submit a grant application to a funder just because there are similar interests between your organization and the funder. In fact, it is important to have a differentiating factor about your organization that can't be articulated within the grant process. The question you must answer is what makes your organization different? How will you highlight the difference? How do you explain the difference in your culture so that it's naturally a part of who you are? Or is that different already in existence within a culture and it needs to be defined it so that others can understand it? These questions are important to answer before you apply for a grant application, let alone complete one.

Another strategy organizations decide to employ is submitting a grant application in partnership with another organization. In a previous section, we talked about leveraging partners to handle your own grant application. You should also consider that there will be times when your organization will not be the lead applicant and will need to choose another organization to submit the lead application for a grant. In some instances, this is a smart strategy. One reason to consider this is, another organization may have the respect and the leverage with a funder that you may not have. For the sake of your organization, the goal is to attach yourself to a winning grant application partner so you can increase the chances of your organization being awarded a piece of a grant as opposed to nothing. The goal is to be awarded something. The reasons the other organization has leverage does not matter. However, what does matter is that you recognize it and the partner organization also recognizes it.

It is worth repeating...for the sake of your organization, the goal is to attach yourself to a winning grant application so you can increase the chances of your organization being awarded a piece of a grant as opposed to nothing. The goal is to be awarded something. It is better to be awarded something that is a part of a larger thing as opposed to nothing at all. In other words, it is more valuable to be awarded 33% of a watermelon than 100% of a grape. As you can tell by the imagery of that example, there is no comparison. Partnership can lead to the survival of an organization. The 33% can represent hundreds of thousands of dollars that you would not have had access to otherwise. The goal when preparing a grant application is to win and be awarded those funds.

Another strategy when preparing a grant application is determining whether you should be the lead or a co-applicant to a grant. In fact, there are some cases in which the best strategy is to not apply at all but to befriend and become a key partner with Strategic

Planning for Nonprofits, who has a likelihood of winning the grant award. In many instances, winning grants creates budgetary line items for subcontractor services that must be provided throughout the grant. This may, in fact, be different from a co-applicant because a co-applicant is held equally responsible for the scope of work that was created by the funder. However, a subcontractor is not necessarily held by the same standard set forward by the funder. Instead, a subcontractor is hired to perform a specific service that may represent 10 or 15% or more of the overall work the lead applicant is responsible for. And in some cases, your nonprofit may decide to make the strategic decision that you take on a subcontractor role and perform a specific service so that your organization can earn that 10 or 15%. The benefit of a subcontractor role in this case is your nonprofit will not have to incur all the overhead that is normally associated with being a leader or co-applicant. In fact, being a subcontractor allows you to perform services like a consultant. The consultant performs specific services and ends their engagement. Many consultants don't have high overhead. And if done correctly and efficiently, a consultant can perform their work without having to spend a lot of money and can return to their normal services where they can generate even more money for the organization. It goes without saying that consultant services may have a higher profit margin that is more attractive. For example, a consultant may charge $100 for services but the cost for those services may in fact be $10. The profit margin in this example is 90%. However, a grant applicant, whether it is the lead or a co-applicant, may charge $100 to a funder to perform a scope of work but the cost of performance of services may be $90. The profit margin in this case is 10%. As you can see by the simple numbers, the profit margin does matter when making strategic decisions to apply or not apply for a grant. Be thoughtful about which makes the most sense for your organization but do not create a blanket approach if you can help it. Not every situation demands a consultant-like approach. Remember to be thoughtful about how you release your resources and your name recognition for such decisions as these.

No matter the strategy you decide to use when submitting a grant application, you should know that every strategy does not apply to every situation. I encourage you to have a flexible approach to each new funding and grant opportunity. Get a good grasp of what the funder is looking for, determine if the grant opportunity is the right fit for your organization, and if you determine your organization should move forward, determine which strategy you should employ to present the best application possible.

CHAPTER 8 - STANDARD GRANT APPLICATION

Developing a standard grant application is one of the smartest things you can do during the process of pursuing grants. A lot of activity takes place when an organization decides to pursue grants. Some of the activity includes finding out as much information as possible from the funder, determining the fit of the grant to your organization's overall strategy, identifying partners who are essential to creating a strong grant application, and other things.

One of the most amazing resources that can help an organization manage its time when it comes to putting together a winning application is developing and maintaining a standard grant application. A standard grant application is a form that replicates most grant applications that exist. The standard grant application created by an organization maintains key information about the organization and about the strategy that will likely be asked by all the funders you will inevitably pursue. Since a lot of this information is similar, your organization needs to ensure that a standard application exists and that it is tweaked when new information becomes available about your organization.

A basic grant application contains the following key components.[ii]

PART 1 - BASIC INFORMATION

1. Legal name of the organization
2. Phone number
3. Address
4. Key contact person (CEO or the person completing the grant application) and their contact information
5. Mission and purpose of your organization
6. Geographic area served
7. Number of individuals served annually, and the % of people served in the specific service area of the funder
8. Number of employees and their employment status (FT or PT) and their ethnic and gender breakdown

9. Board composition - number of board members, ethnic and gender break down, years served

10. Is this for a new program

11. The amount of money requested and for which program year (typically provided by the funder)

12. Your organization's total budget

13. The proposed budget for the project you're requesting funding for

14. Your fiscal year

15. A copy of your 501c3 letter from the IRS

16. Signatures of key staff members and board members

17. An action plan, strategy document, or theory of change associated with the grant application

18. A narrative to answer to series of questions.

PART 2 – A NARRATIVE EXPLAINING YOUR ORGANIZATION

1. Brief summary of organization's history, mission and goals

2. Description of current programs and accomplishments

3. Population the agency benefits: socio-economic status, language, age, physical abilities and/or other descriptions, as appropriate, and how your organization involves them in its planning process

4. How this agency uses volunteers

5. How this agency works with others providing similar services

6. How often did the board of directors meet and the average attendance rate

7. The type of internal financial/accounting controls the organization follows

8. The submission of the most recently completed audit

9. What financial information is given to the board and how often is it provided

10. What is the process used to annually evaluate your organization's executive director

PART 3 – A NARRATIVE EXPLAINING WHY YOU

1. Statement of community needs/issues to be addressed; description of target population to benefit

2. Description of project goals for which funds are being requested

3. Project description, including objectives, activities, timeframe, number served and frequency

4. Description of how the people expected to benefit from this project have been or will be involved in its development and implementation

5. Description of how you plan to evaluate the success of the project, including outcomes and results

6. List of key individuals involved in the project; brief summaries of their qualifications (no resumes, please)

7. How evaluation results will be used for program planning—for both the organization and for others doing similar work

8. Long-term strategies for funding this project beyond the grant period

PART 4 – BUDGET AND FINANCIAL INFORMATION

1. Budget for this grant request showing income and expenses

2. Listing of the funding sources for this request (foundations, corporations, others) solicited for this request for the current year, and, if this is not a new project, for previous years (indicate the amounts requested and status of your proposal with each one)

3. Organization's annual operating budget and actual income-and-expenses for most recently completed fiscal year (align these side by side).

4. Organization's annual operating budget and actual year-to-date income-and-expenses for current year (align these side by side). Please

also include funders, amounts granted and purpose of each grant.

5. Most recent annual financial statement (audited, if available) and management letter (if available).

PART 5 - OTHER SUPPORTING MATERIALS

1. Organizational chart
2. Board membership list with names and affiliations
3. Copy of IRS determination letter and/or explanation of your tax-exempt status
4. Annual Report
5. Letters of agreement, if this is a collaborative proposal (not letters of support)
6. Copy of organizational insurance

As you see by the questions from this standard application, planning every step of the application process helps your organization develop a winning application and, more importantly, it helps you develop a standard winning grant application that can be used repeatedly. Developing a standard grant application will save you time and money.

Another item I want to point out about the standard grant application is the simplicity of the application. Most grant applications are not complex, but some applications will have complex instructions. However, what you should gather from the standard application is, the centralization of basic information is important. Information like your tax ID number or the contact information for key people or the strategy of the organization. This information should be readily available at all times so that an application for grant funds can be completed with as little distraction and fewer stops along the way as possible.

CHAPTER 9 – WHAT YOU SHOULD KNOW MISSION, VISION, GOALS

Your mission, vision, and goals should be clear. These provide a window into the soul of your organization for people who do not know your organization. As you put together a grant application, be aware that these applications are designed to gain a better understanding of your organization. On a grant application, you may not find a request for your mission, vision, and goals. But you may find other questions that hint at the same content that can be found in your mission, vision, and goals. For example, a funder may ask that you provide a theory of change and provide a narrative document that explains the theory of change.[iii] The first column (to the far left) asks "what is the problem you're looking to solve?" For some nonprofits, the answer to the question can be found in their mission, vision, and/or goals. The next few columns ask, "Who is your key audience?" and, "What steps are needed to bring change?" Again, the answer to these questions may be found in the mission, vision, and/or goals.

The point I want to drive home is, having a solid mission, vision, and defined goals makes it easier to complete various key portions of a grant application. Before you prepare a grant application, spend quality time with your leadership team and your board of directors to ensure the best mission, vision, and goal(s) statement(s) are drafted that best represent the organization. This will save you a lot time when drafting an application.

HAVE GOOD DATA

There is no winning grant application without good data. One of the biggest mistakes you could make is to not have good data to support your application.

You can collect good data from the work already completed by others in the market place and by researchers.

As you start achieving results in your program, be sure to purchase and manage a database. Maintain your data in a central location and don't use Microsoft excel.

ANSWER THE QUESTIONS

The purpose of a grant application is for the funder and their reviewers to get to know your organization better. The application and its various sections are designed to gather deeper intelligence that can inform funding decisions. You must keep in mind that all funding decisions are, in fact, an investment in your organization and the work it has proposed to do with the money it receives.

To that end, this next tip gets to the heart of what it means to prepare an effective grant application. That tip is to answer the questions that are asked of your organization directly. The questions are important - as stated earlier. Do what is expected of you and answer those questions. Don't beat around the bush, don't create a fictional story; don't toot your own horn. Just answer the questions.

Some of the challenges people have answering questions are as follows:

1. The person writing the grant does not know the answer to the question relative to the organization.

2. The person writing the grant is too wordy and struggles to get to the point.

3. The persons contributing to the grant provide way too much information making it difficult for the grant writer to determine what to include.

4. The grant writer does not know how to synthesize information collected to answer the question.

5. The organization has a poor history of performance and is trying to answer the questions in ways that do not indict their performance from the past.

6. The organization has a poor history of tracking data and is trying to compensate for the lack of information that has not been collected and managed over a defined period of time.

7. The organization (or someone on staff) is a novice at writing grants.
8. The organization is new to the grant process of a new funder.

These thoughts are not all-inclusive and nor do they represent the challenges organizations face when it comes to answer the questions that are posed in grant applications. But they do point to the challenges associated with answering questions in a grant application.

The answers to these questions can either lead to a winning grant application or a failed grant application.

WORD COUNT

We all think we have awesome ideas and that we need to share those ideas with the world. In fact, some people utilize the grant application process to communicate their awesome ideas, believing these ideas will lead to the award of a new grant for their organization. However, what people do not realize is that when sharing these awesome ideas, funders still have specific requirements that cover the development of a successful grant application. One of those requirements is the word count for each section of the grant. The word count is used to limit the number of words every applicant is allowed to write for each section of the grant. There are many logical and well thought out reasons behind this request by most funders, but it's important for you as the preparer of a grant to embrace the idea that word count does matter - no matter how awesome your idea is.

The logic behind word count varies from funder to funder but here are a couple of concepts that may help you understand the philosophy behind limiting the word count for each section.

Some grant applications are very long and detailed. Limiting the number of words per section allows the grantee to have some control over the review process and limit the amount of time that is spent reviewing the various number of grant applications that will be submitted.

Funders have experience working with organizations that are very wordy about their programs but are never successful in getting to the point of describing their programs. Funders want to support programs and want to invest in programs, but they often find it difficult to understand what they are getting ready to invest in because some organizations are incapable of getting to the point. Limiting the word count for sections throughout the grant application allows the funder to help the organization get to the point as fast and succinct as possible.

Pay attention to the various sections of the grant application. You may notice that some sections may have a lower word count, but a lot of sections may have a higher word count. This is a clear distinction of importance the funder is placing on certain sections of the grant application. While a certain section may have fewer word count acquirements, you still are on the hook for answering those questions effectively. Conversely, sections that have a higher word count should not be taken advantage of.

ACCURATE BUDGET

An accurate budget is so important. A budget tells the story of your program - what the program will accomplish, how it will be accomplished, and who will accomplish it. The strategy you want to employ here is to tell your story and you can do that through the numbers.

FOLLOW DIRECTIONS

At the end of the day, it's imperative for all organizations who are writing a grant proposal to follow the instructions that are provided by the funder. These instructions are essential for the development of the application. They help the funder during the review process determine if the grant application they are looking at is quality, sufficient and is detailed and accurate in what is provided in writing. Any deviation from the instructions the funder provides distracts your application from receiving an honest assessment.

Unlike the greeting that takes place in schools, a funder relies on grant applications to be uniform in their delivery and presentation. It's easy for a funder to see the non-uniform delivery of your application when you do not follow the instructions, and determine that your grant application, in its entirety, is disqualified from further review. When you consider the number of requests a funder receives throughout the year, you can understand why it's important for a funder to receive grant applications that follow the instructions provided. In the process of grant review, unqualified applications are, in most cases, dismissed and not given a fair shot. To avoid this and to keep your application from being dismissed, you must follow instructions.

If you ever wonder what a competitive advantage looks like when completing a grant application, you've found it. The competitive advantage is listed at the top of each grant application as well as throughout the application. The competitive advantage is written in black-and-white and in some cases is no longer than a couple of sentences. The competitive advantage I'm talking about is the set of instructions provided within every grant application.

If a funder may request that you provide 10 printed copies of a grant application you've developed and to deliver them bound in three ring binders, it is your responsibility to ensure that this happens. If your funder requires that all grant applications are signed by the appropriate organization authorities in blue ink, it is your responsibility to ensure that it happens. If your funder requires that your grant application is to be a 12-point font and printed on white paper, not cream paper, it is your responsibility to ensure that this happens. If you know these instructions exist, you should also know that there will always be organizations that are competing with you who will read the same instructions. They are betting that you will not follow these instructions so that their application will have an increased chance of being successful. You should be thinking the same thing. If you are completing a successful grant application, your success is due in part to following instructions. There will be organizations competing against you who will not follow instructions and will, therefore, take themselves out of the running even before the review process commences.

It's imperative that you develop a culture within your organization that values following instructions, particularly from individuals who have leadership or financial leverage over the organization. If the funder has financial leverage of your organization because of its capacity to find or sustain your work or diversify the support of your work, it's a good idea to follow their instructions. What many nonprofit professionals do not consider is that one funder may open the door to many other funders. Funders have conversations with other funders and they communicate thoughts and opinions with each other. If your organization is high-performing and able to follow instructions, that information spreads and may open doors for you to be funded by new funders who you did not consider or who you may not have had prior access to. Opportunities like that come as a result of simply following instructions.

Similarly, opportunities can be lost because your organization refuses to follow instructions. Funders communicate with each other and will tell each other if an organization is low-performing and does not follow simple instructions that are provided in writing. It is essential that you honor these instructions and take advantage of them as a competitive advantage for the sake of your organization, for the sake of your program, and for the sake of the clients you serve.

SECTION 3 - WHAT FUNDERS ARE LOOKING FOR

CHAPTER 10 - IDEAS AND INNOVATION[iv]

Innovation is essential to becoming sustainable. In later chapters, I will discuss the specific areas where nonprofits should spend their time innovating, but in this chapter, I would like to explore innovation in a deeper way. Introducing innovation to an organization can be challenging because innovation is the opportunity to grow a business, survive the difficult times, and significantly influence the direction of an industry. The success of innovation is dependent upon establishing a culture of innovation and a team that leads innovation activities. A culture of innovation encourages the development of ideas that advance the organization. The success of a culture of innovation is measured by its impact on the organization. Impact is determined by how the business has changed or evolved to accommodate innovation. Maintaining a culture of innovation frees management to survey the integration of innovation with the organizational strategy and monitor the outcomes of innovation activities. Innovation has a higher chance for success when a designated group of individuals is responsible for coordinating innovation activities on demand. These activities serve as critical portions of an organization's infrastructure in executing its core business. With the support of an executive sponsor, this team pursues opportunities to determine which ideas can be converted to true innovation. Making this determination makes the difference between an organization becoming or maintaining a sustainable business model and a market leader. At the center of innovation teams are collaborative relationships that have the following the characteristics:

1. Strategic integration—discussing broad goals.
2. Tactical integration—developing plans for specific projects.
3. Operational integration—executing day-to-day tasks.
4. Interpersonal integration—building and sustaining the future of the relationship.
5. Cultural integration—communication skills and cultural awareness to bridge differences.

Innovation leadership is equally as important as having a team that leads innovation activities. A leader of innovation possesses aspirations that challenge complacency and demands the organization to go beyond its current performance, to search, create, and surprise the customer. This type of leadership makes the difference between innovation that is mediocre or transformational. Further, these leaders possess the following characteristics:

1. A vision that tells the organization where it is going. The vision establishes a parameter for ongoing innovation activities. The parameter differentiates which activities are relevant to the organization's long-term strategy.

2. A commitment to innovation by way of resources. Resources encompass finances, tools, and teams to complete the work. The combination of these resources counts as a significant investment toward making innovation a significant portion of an organization's strategy.

3. An innovation strategy and a set of processes and management systems to support the strategy.
4. Leading by example.
5. A clear sense of command and responsibility for making tough decisions.
6. Receptive to new ideas and change.

CHAPTER 11 - STABILITY IN LEADERSHIP, FINANCES, AND PERFORMANCE

Every little thing about your organization can make the difference between a winning grant application and a losing one. Stability in the following areas is evaluated and considered by funders - (1) leadership, (2) finances, and (3) performance.

Leadership stability is important for an organization's ability to fulfill its mission and overall purpose. If an organization has constant turn over, particularly among its senior leadership, it signals to stakeholders that the organization is unable to retain talent or does a bad job of selecting top tier talent that can manage organizational and programmatic operations. Finding and retaining talent to manage organizational and programmatic operations puts funders and stakeholders at ease. When funders know - without a shadow of doubt - that their investment in your organization will be overseen (stewarded) by capable hands who know how to deploy those resources to meet the goals proposed in a winning grant application, they are more likely to grant funds. Similarly, as a leader who is looking to get better at grant writing, consider how your leadership impacts a grant application. Consider how your leadership influences a decision on a grant application you are associated with. You may be asking, "How does leadership impact a grant application?" When you consider the other components of a grant application funders look for - in some cases - the resumes (or biographies) of the executive leaders and program managers who will be associated are looked at. When this information is passed along with a grant application, know that funders are looking at your past performance and capabilities as a contributor or perhaps as the lead person for this potential grant. You may have thought your resume was only relevant for obtaining new employment, however, funders look to resumes to get a sense of the type of quality that is obtained by the organization applying for funding and a sense of innovative leadership that ensures the funds granted are used appropriately and maximized for the benefit of the clients who will be served. At the end of the day, you have to look at a grant application as an opportunity to sell your organization to someone who is interested in investing in your organization. If you do a poor job selling yourself, you cannot expect to obtain a new investor or retain old investors. Sales includes selling leadership stability to a funder who is trusting their funding to someone other than himself.

Let me make a note here, your resume will go a long way toward describing a few things about you and your team members.

1. The presence or absence of sound leadership qualities
2. Disengaged leadership
3. Immature leadership
4. Strategic leadership

Your resume tells the full story about your leadership. What is your story?

CHAPTER 12 - A RESUME OF RESULTS

Not only do the resumes of the leaders and program staff matter, the resume of your organization matters. What is the resume of your organization? Your organization's resume is no different than the resume of individuals looking for employment. For the sake of this example, let's talk about what's included in a resume.

- Objective statement = Mission statement
- Professional skills = Core competency
- Education = Existing skills and training or theory of change for your proposal
- Experience = Programs under operations and performance
- Board affiliations = Memberships and Roundtable membership
- References = Letters of support

As you can see, there's a direct correlation between a standard resume and the resume of your organization.

When you're submitting a grant application, you will not be asked to submit a resume in a standard fashion like you would for a job interview, but you will be asked questions about your organization's resume in one way or another throughout the application. But rest assured that your resume will speak volumes to the funder. You should also know that your reputation in the community will come to bear as well. When I speak of community, I'm not speaking about the location where your organization serves clients. When I speak of community, I'm speaking about other service providers and stakeholders who have received or observed the services you provide to clients. Similar to references that are provided during a job interview, stakeholders and partners who have experienced your services or have observed your services are clear references who can bolster your resume. In some instances, these references speak louder than your application. You'll be surprised that these references will share stories about what you are capable of doing, and not doing well, before you submit the application. In this instance, you are not aware of how your story is being told. You may have been telling it but funders hear other stories and they are making judgment calls based upon the stories they hear. If a funder trusts the word coming from a particular stakeholder or partner, that story can hold a lot of weight.

Similarly, if the story is told by someone a funder does not trust and respect, that story will not hold a lot of weight. You can do the math and see with your own eyes but let me just share this piece of advice. It's better to be a high performer who is consistent and known for providing reliable services than try to get people to tell your story on your behalf. You have no idea who knows you or how people might be telling your story. You don't even have an idea how people are perceiving your story. Needless to say, this is also true when you're applying for a job. The best solution to this is to be consistent so that regardless of who's telling a story, the same story, or some version of the same story, is being told in your absence. Those patterns and similarities will be picked up by funders and it says a lot about who you are when no one is looking.

CHAPTER 13 - OTHER FUNDING PARTNERS

Funders listen to other funders who are also investing in the project you are proposing. There aren't many funders who are willing to be the only funder for a project. In fact, if we talk to funders, big or small, they will tell you that they value the investments of other funders in a project. The reason they like this is, other funders provide stability and credibility to the work proposed. If you are unable to convince another funder to support your work, it does say a lot about you and speaks to the lack of credibility you may have in the nonprofit community.

You may be saying to me right now, "I just need to get my first funding partner on board." And if you're saying this to me right now, you're correct. But let me share with you that simply getting your first funding partner can be a challenge, particularly if you are just starting out. This is no different than when you're trying to get your first job. You had to convince someone to hire you even if you didn't have the right experience or enough experience. One of the oldest tricks in the book that jobseekers use to let employers know that they are a credible employee and a worthwhile investment is to show work history. Even if the work history is unpaid, work history is valuable. Jobseekers who are just starting out in their careers or who just graduated from college may seek out opportunities to be a volunteer or intern for the experience alone. The more internships and volunteer opportunities individuals can show in their resume, the more of a work history they can show. And when this job seeker is finally ready to apply for an opportunity that suits their interest in your required skill set, they can. Back to the volunteer opportunities and the internship opportunities they took to take advantage of to gain valuable work experience. The same concept works in the nonprofit community. If you are not able to generate revenue on your own by winning and grant applications, it might be in your best interest to volunteer as a sub-grantee on another grant. In this case, you may not get paid or you may get paid very little. However, the goal is not compensation. The goal is to gain valuable project experience on a major grant that has high visibility among stakeholders and funders who may later be funding projects you are the lead on. You may be asking, "How do I find these projects?" The way to find projects that are funded by serious funders and have high visibility is as follows:

1. Identify your core area of performance
2. Find out who the major players (organizations) are
3. Identify key staff members you can realistically schedule a meeting with
4. Offer your organization to volunteer on the project to conduct key tasks
5. Give your all and participate in every activity you can, including team meetings, writing reports, attending site visits, etc.
6. Perform the tasks assigned to you
7. Keep track of your contributions and successes
8. Ask permission to report on your contributions to key decisions makers
9. Ask for a reference

SECTION 4 - TIDBITS TO IMPROVE YOUR GRANT WRITING

CHAPTER 14 – TIPS AND TRICKS THAT MAKE A DIFFERENCE

1. **INCLUDE YOUR TEAM IN THE WRITING PROCESS -** Your team is your best asset. Use them. Here are a few reasons you should include your team in the writing process.

   - They have a working knowledge of programs and the needs of clients.

   - They understand the nuances of program operations that can lead to the development of innovative solutions.

   - Their work is your resume and that resume (story) needs to be told from their eyes.

   - They have stories that can add color to a grant application to make it a winning grant application.

2. **EDUCATE YOUR TEAM ABOUT FUNDERS -** The more your team knows about the funders that pay their salaries, the more

they will understand how funds are raised, how budgets are formulated and managed, and how funders monitor progress along the way. Here are a few reasons you want to educate your team about funders.

- Leaders cannot be present at all times, but an informed staff can display continuity in the absence of a leader.

- Decisions are made throughout the life cycle of a grant and an informed staff can make the adjustment process smoother than normal.

- Broadening your staff's exposure to the expectations of funders broadens the thought process of staff members as they execute their jobs.

3. **CELEBRATE GRANT AWARDS (BIG OR SMALL)** - All grant awards are important. While larger grants are the Holy Grail for all nonprofits, the smaller grants are just as important to the sustainability to your organization. The little grants of $5000 or

$10,000 or $20,000 can be the missing key to meeting payroll or ensuring program continuity. Here are additional reasons to celebrate grant awards.

- All grants are a blessing and a resource.
- Each successful grant application offers a lesson learned to improve the development of the next grant application.
- Small grant awards create a resume of success that can be leveraged for pursuing and successfully obtaining larger grant awards.
- Small grant funders have relationships with large grantors and can be your references to a much larger grant opportunity.

4. **ASK FOR FEEDBACK BETWEEN DRAFTS -** Writing a grant application in a silo is never a good idea. In fact, before writing a grant application, you should strongly consider engaging in a writing session. Writing sessions allow the best ideas to come to life. Those ideas may turn into a winning application. Here are

some additional reasons to ask for feedback between drafts.

- Feedback allows your application to improve.
- Some feedback allows others to speak words of affirmation.
- Some feedback allows others to speak words of critique - which may be the right feedback you need to hear to stop the submission of a bad application and a bad idea.
- Feedback can add nuance and color to an application that may be missing the one ingredient that can make a difference between winning and losing an award.

5. **STEWARD EXISTING GRANTS** - Nonprofit leaders are always on the lookout for the next grant opportunity. This is with good reason. Like any other business, nonprofits need income and cash flow to keep their doors open, to keep staff paid, and to cover overhead costs. However, there are times when nonprofit

leaders can forget about minding the store or stewarding existing grants. There are a couple of thoughts about why stewarding existing grants is equally important to obtaining new funding.

- An existing Grant is evidence that your organization has the ability to write a winning application.

- Existing money can lead to new funding from the same source.

- Existing money can lead to leveraging funding from other resources and partners.

- Existing money signals to other funders that your organization may be a safe investment of their money.

- Existing money allows your organization to forecast how it will operate.

6. **BE AWARE OF, NOT WARY OF, COMPETITION** - All businesses have competition. This is especially true in the nonprofit community. If you look around the geographic location of nonprofits, you will

notice that nonprofits are typically huddled in specific communities to meet the specific needs of a specific client base. In many instances, nonprofits are serving the same clients. With this said, here are a few thoughts about why you should be aware of, but not wary of, competition:

- Competition will tell you the importance of the topic your organization is focused on.

- Competition may, in fact, detract from your ability to serve the number of clients you plan to serve.

- Competition may step in and take away funding you thought you had.

- Competition will challenge you to do better and be better in your delivery.

- In some instances, funders will force you to work with your competition because funders know that leveraging resources from multiple organizations is a better use of funds then giving an entire part to just one organization.

7. **MAINTAIN A CULTURE OF PERFORMANCE** - The culture of your organization is important. The culture has a direct impact on the outcomes your organization achieves. In fact, a dysfunctional culture can disrupt organizational performance. To achieve results that matter on a regular basis, your organization's culture has to be created to yield these results. Here are a few ways to establish and maintain a culture of performance:

- Set a cultural standard that demands performance excellence and meets the goals of the program.
- Be consistent in maintaining those standards.
- Hold yourself accountable to the same standards.
- Remove distractions and detractions that negatively impact what you're building within your organization.

8. **WORK WITH PARTNERS** - Partners can make a difference in the success of your organization. Partners can add value to your program by bringing critical assets like money, clients, connections, etc. If you have the right set of partners, your program and your clients will stand to benefit the most. Here are a few ways to find and secure partners:

- Have a clear understanding of the services you are providing to and for your clients.

- Identify which of those services are your clear core competency (where your strength is).

- When you determine what you're not good at, find partners who are good at it so you can close that gap.

- Be sure to identify several prospects.

- Develop a measurement tool to determine how to qualify a prospect as a strong potential partner.

- Schedule face-to-face meetings with their team and yours.

- Fill out your measurement tool and make a solid decision.
- Complete a MOU with the selected partners.
- If possible, select several partners - even if it's for the same service.
- Manage the relationship to ensure performance is achievable.

9. **CREATE AN INTERNAL GRANT WRITING PROCESS -** No one person can write a winning grant on their own. It takes a team of people to contribute to the development of a winning grant application. While there is one main person who writes the grant, the team makes the grant writing process a success. Here are few tips for developing a grant writing process:

- Clearly identify the grant writer.
- Clearly identify contributors to the grant writing process.
- Develop a template for capturing ideas and thoughts.

- Schedule writing sessions for people to write and present their ideas.
- Generate a winning grant application from this writing session.
- Solicit feedback from writing session contributors to learn how to improve the process.

10. **SEARCH FOR GRANTS** - Searching for grants can be a frustrating process. Many people do not know where to look or how to get started. Here are a few thoughts on how simplify and improve the grant search process:

- Identify a grant database website.
- Sign up for grant list services.
- Maintain relationships with providers who are winning grants and learn how they discover meaningful grant opportunities.
- Partner with other providers to pursue grants together.

OTHER RESOURCES

GRANT DATABASES

- www.foundationcenter.org
- www.grants.gov
- www.grantwatch.com
- www.grantforward.com

RESOURCES FROM THE AUTHOR

- Author website: www.drwilliampclark.com
- Other books and resources by the author:
  www.gumroad.com/drwilliampclark
- Consulting services: www.elipatrick.com

ABOUT THE AUTHOR

Dr. William Clark has over 15 years of experience working in city government, nonprofit administration and public housing operations.

In 2017, Dr. Clark joined Career Resources Inc. (CRI) as the Vice President of Strategic Initiatives with oversight of statewide operations of workforce development training programs and organizational sustainability initiatives. In this role, Dr. Clark has raised millions of dollars in grant funding.

Prior to joining CRI, Dr. Clark served as the Director of Workforce Solutions Collaborative of Metro Hartford. In 18 months, he oversaw a team that raised over $2 million in grant funding, helped job seekers served earn an occupational skill certification in the healthcare, manufacturing, or transportation sector, and assisted 6 out of 10 jobseekers obtain a good job with family sustaining wages.

Prior to joining Workforce Solutions, Dr. Clark served as Director of Special Projects for the City of Philadelphia's Office of Economic Opportunity where he was responsible for over $4.5 billion of Economic Opportunity Plans (EOPs), ensuring supplier, employment, and job seeker diversity for major construction projects.

Dr. Clark is a lecturer and the author of several books on nonprofit and church leadership including Leadership Development for Nonprofits and Sustainability: Developing a sustainable faith-based or nonprofit organization. He is also the author of several personal development books, including: Leverage: Taking advantage of your right now to build your tomorrow.

In addition to his many responsibilities, Dr. Clark is the lead pastor of Living Faith Church in Hartford CT.

Dr. Clark holds a Doctor of Strategic Leadership degree from Regent University and a Master of Leadership Development degree from Penn State University.

AUTHOR CONTACT INFORMATION

Web: www.drwilliampclark.com

Email: drwilliampclark@gmail.com

Social Media: @DrWilliamPClark

END NOTES

---

[i] http://www.alliancemagazine.org/blog/non-profit-performance-evaluation-leverage-part-4-of-6

[ii] https://www.ctphilanthropy.org/sites/default/files/resources/Common%20Grant%20Application%20Form_0.docx

[iii] Sample theory of change: http://diytoolkit.org/tools/theory-of-change

[iv] Sustainable: Developing A Sustainable Faith-Based or Nonprofit Organization

www.ingramcontent.com/pod-product-compliance
Lightning Source LLC
Chambersburg PA
CBHW021717210326
41599CB00013B/1683